LOUISE BORDEN

SEA CLOCKS

THE STORY OF LONGITUDE

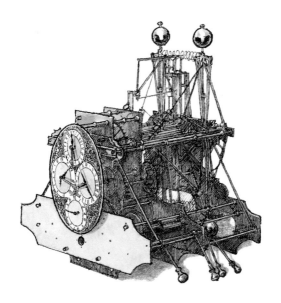

ILLUSTRATED BY

ERIK BLEGVAD

MARGARET K. McELDERRY BOOKS

NEW YORK   LONDON   TORONTO   SYDNEY   SINGAPORE

ALSO BY LOUISE BORDEN
AMERICA IS . . .
THE DAY EDDIE MET THE AUTHOR
FLY HIGH! THE STORY OF BESSIE COLEMAN
SLEDS ON BOSTON COMMON: A STORY FROM THE AMERICAN REVOLUTION
GOOD LUCK, MRS. K!
GOOD-BYE, CHARLES LINDBERGH
THE LITTLE SHIPS: THE HEROIC RESCUE AT DUNKIRK IN WORLD WAR II
TOUCHING THE SKY: THE FLYING ADVENTURES OF WILBUR AND ORVILLE WRIGHT

ACKNOWLEDGMENTS
With grateful thanks to Dava Sobel, Will Andrewes, Jonathan Betts, and Andrew King
for their encouragement and expertise in reading drafts of this book.
DAVA SOBEL is the author of several books, including the well-known *Longitude* (Walker and Co., 1995).
WILLIAM J. H. ANDREWES has served as the David P. Wheatland Curator of the Collection of
Historical Scientific Instruments at Harvard University, and edited *The Quest for Longitude*
(Collection of Historical Scientific Instruments, 1996).
JONATHAN BETTS currently serves as Curator of Horology at the National Maritime Museum in
Greenwich, England, and has authored several texts about John Harrison.
ANDREW KING is a clockmaker and lives in Beckenham, Kent, England.
Thanks also to Maryann Macdonald, and to Leah Bohrer and her third and fourth grade students.

Margaret K. McElderry Books
An imprint of Simon & Schuster Children's Publishing Division
1230 Avenue of the Americas
New York, New York 10020

Text copyright © 2004 by Louise Borden
Illustrations copyright © 2004 by Erik Blegvad
All rights reserved, including the right of reproduction in
whole or in part in any form.

Book design by Michael Nelson
The text for this book is set in Baskerville.
The illustrations are rendered in watercolor.

Manufactured in China
1 2 3 4 5 6 7 8 9 10

LIBRARY OF CONGRESS CATALOGING-IN-PUBLICATION DATA
Borden, Louise.
Sea clocks : the story of longitude / by Louise Borden;
illustrated by Erik Blegvad.
p. cm.
ISBN 0-689-84216-3
1. Chronometers—History—Juvenile literature.
2. Longitude—Measurement—History—Juvenile literature.
3. Harrison, John, 1693-1776—Juvenile literature.
4. Clock and watch makers—Great Britain—Biography—
Juvenile literature. [I. Harrison, John, 1693-1776.
2. Inventors. 3. Clocks and watches. 4. Longitude.]
I. Blegvad, Erik, ill. II. Title.
QB107 B75 2003
526'.62'09—dc21
00-045599

FIRST
EDITION

for Sydney
who is always on time for my train

and

for Dava Sobel

—L. B.

THIS STORY IS ABOUT A MAN FROM LINCOLNSHIRE, ENGLAND, who spent over forty years of his life

making strange and beautiful sea clocks.

Five of them!

This story is also about famous astronomers

and scientists

and ship captains

and kings

and a big and important problem

that no one could solve for hundreds of years. . . .

The English clockmaker's name was John Harrison.

One of his five sea clocks was very special—

it changed the world in a wonderful way.

But, *before* those clocks,

this story begins with the important events

of John Harrison's early life.

JOHN HARRISON was born
in March 1693 in
the county of Yorkshire.
His father, Henry,
was a joiner, or carpenter.
His mother was named Elizabeth.
At the age of about four,
John moved with his family
to the county of Lincolnshire.
There they lived in the village of Barrow
on the south bank of the river Humber,
almost two hundred miles north
of the great city of London.

There were five Harrison children.
John was the oldest.
Then came Mary,
then Henry,
then James,
who later helped his brother
build some of his clocks.
And a baby who died.

John Harrison had an ear for music.
He loved to sing.
He could play the viol.
And he was a bell ringer
at the parish church in Barrow.
Pulling on the long ropes that rang the heavy bells
helped him later
when he studied the workings of clocks.

John's father wanted his oldest son
to grow up to be a joiner,
so he taught him all the skills
a good Lincolnshire carpenter
needed to know.

Most important,
when John was a boy,
he had a hunger for books and for learning,
a hunger most other village folk didn't have.
He learned to read and write from his father
because in a river village like Barrow,
there were no schools
and few books.

One day,
a visiting clergyman
loaned him a copy
of a Cambridge University math professor's lectures.
Young John Harrison knew this was a gift
to be kept all his life.

So he copied the lectures,
page by page,
in his small, neat handwriting.
Sometimes he would reread the lectures,
study them,
and make notes in the margins.
He was always thinking,
always pondering,
always asking himself questions
about how mechanical things worked.

As a carpenter,
John Harrison had strong, steady hands
and he knew about different kinds of wood.
Yet somehow,
John grew more interested in building clocks
than in using his skills like an ordinary village carpenter.
He was *not* an ordinary man.

When he was only twenty years old,
John Harrison built his first clock,
mostly of wood.
He signed it with his name and the date.
With his quick mind,
and without any training in clockmaking,
he had figured out the right way
for the wooden wheels and teeth to mesh and turn
in this long-case clock.
It kept good time.

In the next seventeen years,
by 1730,
John Harrison had built at least seven more clocks.
Many of these were very unusual.
Sometimes
his brother James assisted him.
One of the clocks
was for the stables of a Lincolnshire estate.
John Harrison knew that the oil in a clock
often got thick
and stopped the clock's parts from running.
So he built this clock
with parts made from brass
and a greasy kind of wood.
This way his clock didn't need *any* oil to run.

The river Humber was there too,
as an early part of this story.
A few miles away,
across the river from Barrow,
was the great English port of Hull.
Ships from France and Flanders and Holland,
and from the Baltic Sea,
came there to trade.

Maybe it was on the busy docks of this harbor
or on his own village riverbank
that John Harrison heard talk
of a big prize
that would bring money and fame.
The prize had to do with the problem
no one thought could ever be solved.

This was the problem:

For hundreds of years,
ships had been sailing to places far and near
without really knowing where they were!
Kings and queens
and learned men and ship captains
all thought it was the biggest scientific problem
of their time.

When Christopher Columbus and Magellan
and other famous explorers
were sailing across oceans,
they knew their *latitude*,
that is, their location
north or south of the equator.
Any good sailor could figure that out
by where the sun was at noon
or by looking at the Pole Star
(also known as the North Star)
at night.

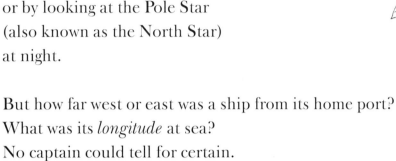

But how far west or east was a ship from its home port?
What was its *longitude* at sea?
No captain could tell for certain.
Seamen had to guess.
They knew about currents,
and shorebirds,
and things like that.
But sometimes
they ended up sailing in the wrong direction.
Or taking too long to get where they were going.
Then the ships ran out of fresh food and water.

Sailors got sick with scurvy
and died.

Sometimes ships got lost in storms;
sometimes they ran aground and sank.
Captains sailed along the same latitude routes
just to be safe.
But pirates knew those routes too.
Rich cargoes and many lives were lost.
Kings and queens were upset.
So were ship captains and merchants.
All because of this problem:
No one could figure out a way to find the longitude at sea.

Famous scientists such as Isaac Newton
knew that the earth was round
and that there were 360 degrees in a circle.
This meant there were 360 degrees of longitude.
By dividing 360 degrees by 24,
the number of hours in a day,
navigators knew that *each hour*
was marked by 15 degrees of longitude.
So . . .

if it was noon on a ship sailing *west*
and 2 P.M. back at the home port,
a captain could tell he was 30 degrees *west*
of that port.
If it was 2 P.M. on a ship sailing *east*
and noon back at the home port,
a captain could tell he was 30 degrees
east of that port.
Time was an important piece of the longitude
and location puzzle.

Newton and navigators
already knew the big problem could be solved
if a ship at sea knew two things:
what time it was onboard that ship,
wherever it was in the world,
and also the exact time back at the home port.
If ship captains knew these two times,
then they could find their longitude.
Sailors could figure out their local ship time
by using the sun and the stars.
But how could a captain know his *home port's* time?

In the 1700s
watches were not good at keeping accurate time
and since they cost a lot of money,
common folk couldn't afford them.
Clocks were better at keeping time,
but clocks were expensive too.

Besides, clocks could not work on a rolling ship.
Clocks had pendulums
that would swing wildly in rough weather.
Also, changes in climate and temperature
affected the way clocks worked.
A clock might keep good time on land,
but at sea,
after being tossed about on a ship,
it would be a poor timekeeper.
So, it was *impossible*
for normal clocks to solve the problem.

But maybe the moon
and its position among the stars could help the navigators
tell the time.
Astronomers in many parts of Europe
thought the answer to the problem
was somewhere in the heavens.
Edmond Halley,
the Astronomer Royal of England,
whose name was later given to a famous comet,
thought so too.

Halley, as well as other astronomers and mathematicians,
studied the moon's motion
night by night,
month by month,
year by year.
But still,
they didn't find the right answer
to the biggest scientific problem of the age.

In 1714
the English Parliament
had voted to award 20,000 pounds sterling
to anyone who could solve the longitude problem.
This was the great prize John Harrison heard about.
20,000 pounds was an *enormous* sum of money!

John Harrison started to think about the big problem
that no one had yet solved;
20,000 pounds would make him rich and famous!
He looked at the wooden clocks in his Barrow workshop
that he and his brother James had made.
Then he pondered
why clocks couldn't keep good time at sea.
Ordinary men might have thought
the longitude problem could never be solved.
But not John Harrison.

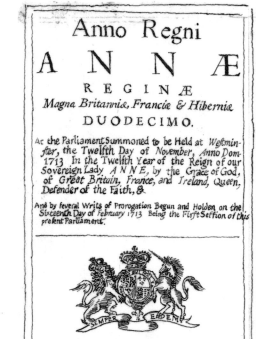

Anno Regni
ANNÆ
REGINÆ
Magna Britanniæ, Franciæ & Hiberniæ
DUODECIMO.

At the Parliament Summoned to be Held at Westmin-
fter, the Twelfth Day of November, Anno Dom.
1713 In the Twelfth Year of the Reign of our
Sovereign Lady ANNE, by the Grace of God,
of Great Britain, France, and Ireland, Queen,
Defender of the Faith, &

And by feveral Writs of Prorogation Begun and Holden on the
Sixteenth Day of February 1713 Being the Firft Seffion of this
prefent Parliament.

LONDON
Printed by John Baskett, Printer to the Queens moft Excellent Majefty, And by the Affigns of Thomas Newcomb,
and Henry Hills, deceas'd. 1714.

He made more notes,
studied his clocks again and again,
and spent long hours in his workshop.
He also talked with his brother James about the differences
between land clocks and sea clocks.
Then he tested different metals
on cold days and warm days
on the outside wall of his house.

Finally,
he drew a design for a special clock,
a clock *without a pendulum*
that could withstand the rocking of a ship at sea.
Its parts would move together in such a way
that temperature wouldn't affect it.
Wherever the clock was on the high seas,
it could still keep excellent time.

Then, taking the plans and illustrations
for the sea clock with him,
John Harrison traveled the long miles
to the great city of London.
This was in 1730.
He went first to the Royal Observatory at Greenwich,
to see Dr. Edmond Halley.
Halley still thought that studying the stars
was the best way to solve the longitude problem.
But he liked this country carpenter John Harrison.
And he liked his plan
for a special sea clock.
So he sent Harrison to see George Graham,
the best watchmaker in London.

George Graham liked the Barrow carpenter too
and his plan for this new and strange clock.
The two craftsmen talked all day.
Then they talked through supper.
When John Harrison left Mr. Graham's house that night,
he left with a promise of friendship
and a loan of money.
George Graham wanted John Harrison to build that clock.
And he wanted him to succeed.

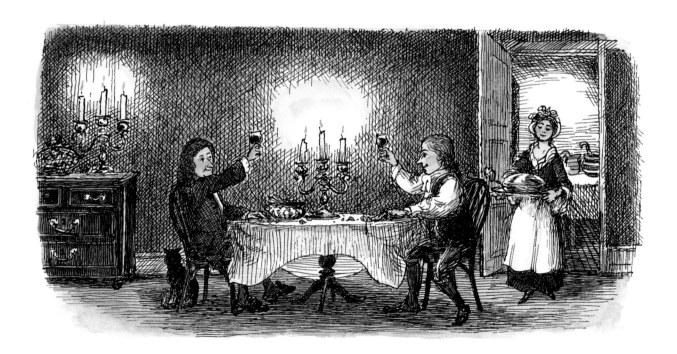

It took John Harrison *five* years to build his sea clock.
His brother James helped him,
and when it was finished,
they tested the timekeeper
on a barge on the river Humber.

This clock was later called H-1.
(The H, of course, stood for Harrison.)
And it was a strange clock indeed.
Its frame was made of brass,
but its wheels and other parts
were made of wood.
When John Harrison took his clock to London
to show to George Graham,
many scientists and important people also
wanted to see it.

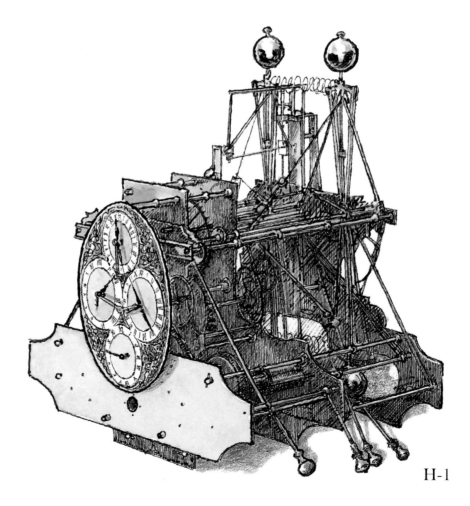

H-1

In May 1736
Harrison sailed with H-1 to Lisbon, Portugal,
aboard the *Centurion,*
to test his clock at sea.
He was dreadfully seasick,
but H-1 ran very well.
On the return from Lisbon aboard the *Orford,*
the ship's captain gave the strange sea clock high marks.
John Harrison told him the ship was sixty-eight miles off course,
and this proved to be correct.
However,
to win the longitude prize,
a clock had to prove itself
onboard a ship sailing
all the way to the West Indies,
about a sixty-day trip!
Also, to win the entire 20,000 pounds
a timekeeper could only lose or gain two minutes
during the entire sea voyage.

Rather than ask the Board of Longitude
to allow H-1 to go on such a trial,
John Harrison asked for money
to help him build a *second* clock.
This one would be slimmer in size,
an even better sea clock!
H-1 in its wood case
had taken up too much space
on the Lisbon trip.
The Board said "Yes" right away.
They were not ready to award John Harrison the prize,
but they felt that his clock held great promise.

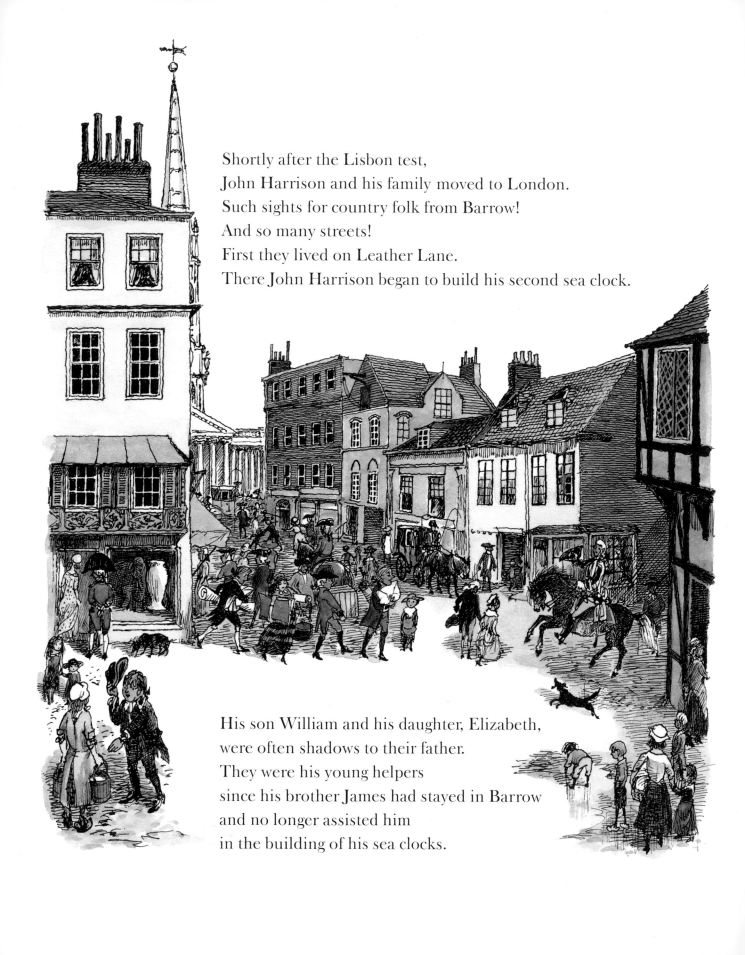

Shortly after the Lisbon test,
John Harrison and his family moved to London.
Such sights for country folk from Barrow!
And so many streets!
First they lived on Leather Lane.
There John Harrison began to build his second sea clock.

His son William and his daughter, Elizabeth,
were often shadows to their father.
They were his young helpers
since his brother James had stayed in Barrow
and no longer assisted him
in the building of his sea clocks.

H-2 was finished in 1739.
John Harrison was forty-six years old.
He would spend the rest of his life
building three more sea clocks
and trying to get the Board of Longitude
to award him the prize that he felt he deserved.

H-2 was never to go to sea.
Already
John Harrison was thinking of a plan
for a third timekeeper,
with even more changes.
But this clock, H-3,
smaller and lighter,
took him *nineteen years* to complete.

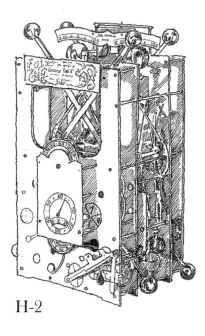

H-2

John Harrison was the kind of man
who never gave up.
He was stubborn in the best kind of way.
He believed in his sea clocks.
And, most importantly,
John Harrison believed in himself
and in his bold, new ideas.
Also, his family believed in him.
They knew that someday
John Harrison's mechanical genius would be recognized.

In 1749,
in the middle of those nineteen years
that it took to build his third sea clock,
the Royal Society
gave John Harrison their highest award,
the famous Copley Gold Medal.
This was to honor John Harrison's hard work
as well as his great contributions to science.
John Harrison had important friends,
who believed in his work as well.

Even though those were lean and difficult years,
John Harrison was no longer an unknown clockmaker.
Often scientists, artists,
and men from all walks of life
came to his house on Red Lion Square,
where the Harrison family now lived,
to look at his clocks.
One of those visitors was the inventor Benjamin Franklin.
This was on December 1, 1757,
the same year the third sea clock was completed.

H-3 didn't weigh as much
as John Harrison's first two sea clocks.
And its inscription was plain:
simply JOHN HARRISON across its face.
H-3 also had two new and important clock features.
Yet John Harrison had some doubts about it.
He called this clock "my curious third machine."
After nineteen years of work,
he wasn't sure it was the best timekeeper
he could design.
He had been thinking about a *watch*,
as a better solution,
rather than a large sea clock.

H-3

Earlier, in 1753,
while still tinkering with his curious third machine,
John Harrison had designed a pocket watch,
and had given the plans to John Jefferys,
a watchmaker who lived a few streets away.
He used the watch that Jefferys made
as his own personal pocket watch.
He took this watch to the Board of Longitude,
asking for more money to support his work.
Harrison told the Board that he would
now try to make a *sea watch,*
a watch that would keep the time
just as well as a clock.
And it would be more practical
than his bigger sea clocks.
Maybe this watch could go on a sea trial *with* H-3.

By now John's son William had grown up
and become his father's right-hand man.
William wasn't the clockmaker that his father was,
or the mechanical thinker.
But he wanted to help John Harrison win that great prize.
William went with his father on his many visits
to the Board of Longitude and sometimes
spoke on his father's behalf.

John Harrison was often in need of money.
The brass and metal parts of his sea clocks,
and the special pieces he used
were very expensive to buy.
Sometimes he paid skilled workmen
to make these parts.
Fortunately,
the Board of Longitude never refused
his requests for money to continue his work.
Harrison had few other jobs;
building these special clocks was his life work.

But the years were moving past,
and the Board began to get tired of waiting
for John Harrison to build the right clock.
Also, he had lost his good friends:
Dr. Halley and George Graham
were no longer alive.

Other mathematicians and astronomers
were now members of the Board.
They had their doubts about a *clockmaker's* solution,
so they weren't as quick to support his ideas and plans.
Over the years,
John Harrison and his son lost trust in these men.

John Harrison was growing old and weary.
His eyesight wasn't as good as it used to be.
His hands weren't as strong and steady.
But John Harrison still had more courage
than all the pompous astronomers and mathematicians put together.
They had each other, with their same old ideas.
But John Harrison had to stand alone for much of his life . . .
searching for an answer
that most of the scientific world had given up on.

He continued to work,
sometimes into the night,
with only a candle by his side for light.
He tinkered
and tested
and pondered.
He studied his notes
and drew up new plans.
And finally his fourth timekeeper was finished.
This was the special clock
that would change the world.
It was different from his sea clocks
in size and looks,
because it was a large, silver *watch*.
Its parts were very small
and needed oil.
But John Harrison designed it so well,
that wasn't a problem.
H-4 was perfect in every way
and it was also beautiful.

H-4

In July of 1760,
when he was sixty-seven years of age,
John Harrison and William met again
with the Board of Longitude.
They asked for a trial at sea for H-3 . . .
and wanted to send H-4 along as well.
They also asked for one more winter of cold weather
to test this new five-and-a-half-inch watch.

It was decided that William would sail on the trial.
There were many delays.
Then more delays.
But John Harrison had spent years making his sea clocks.
He was a patient man.

Finally,
William sailed for the West Indies.
H-4 went with him but not H-3;
John Harrison had decided to send
only his newest timekeeper.

On the voyage to Jamaica,
H-4 performed so well
that the ship's captain
wanted to buy the next watch
John Harrison made.
William was able to determine
the *exact* longitude of the ship
and correct the errors of the navigator onboard.
The return to England was stormy and rough.
William had to wrap blankets around H-4,
to keep it safe and dry.
Even so,
he wound it daily.
William believed in his father's watch
in any kind of weather.
H-4 should have won the prize after this trial.

But the Board of Longitude disagreed.
When Harrison told them that H-4
had lost less than two minutes on the trip,
the Board couldn't believe the watch's success.
It was simply *too* incredible.

This was hard news, indeed,
for John Harrison and his son William.
They knew H-4 was a prizewinning timekeeper.
But how to prove this?
There were several meetings.
And more meetings.
And always
there was bickering.
After all, a great prize was at stake.

Nevil Maskelyne, an English astronomer,
was working hard
to find the longitude solution in the stars.
He didn't think a clock would ever solve the problem.
When H-4 was finally allowed a *second* sea trial to the West Indies,
Nevil Maskelyne sailed in a ship ahead of William's to the West Indies.
He would check H-4's rate himself.

On this second trip,
H-4 was a huge success.
Its error was tiny . . .
three times better
than what was required to win the 20,000 pounds!

But again,
the Board of Longitude denied John Harrison the prize.
Maybe this watch
could not have copies made quickly or cheaply.
Maybe another copy couldn't even be made!
They paid John Harrison 10,000 pounds,
only half the reward,
and they told him they wanted his clocks.
Soon after this,
in 1765,
Nevil Maskelyne became the Astronomer Royal.
Now he had a vote on the Board of Longitude.
This hurt John Harrison's chances of winning
the longitude prize.
The Board told Harrison that he must take apart H-4
and explain to a group of London's best watchmakers
how it worked.
One of them, Larcum Kendall,
was asked by the Board of Longitude
to make a copy of H-4.

It was unfair to take John Harrison's sea clocks,
dismantle them in a rough manner,
and carry them off to the Royal Observatory,
with *no* regard for the damage to them.
This is what happened . . .
thanks to Nevil Maskelyne.
In 1766,
after taking H-4 to Greenwich to be tested and copied,
Maskelyne went to Red Lion Square
and took H-1, H-2, and H-3 as well.
H-1 was dropped and damaged.

John Harrison set to work on H-5,
another watch,
almost identical to H-4.
The Harrisons finished H-5 in 1772,
in John Harrison's eightieth year.

The Board of Longitude had demanded
that John Harrison make *two* more watches.
(H-5 counted as one.)
They now had taken H-4 from him,
as well as his first three clocks.
How could an eighty-year-old man
complete *another* watch
for the Board?
Yet this is what their new rules required
to win the second half of the prize.

Meanwhile,
Larcum Kendall had made his copy of H-4
a few years earlier and it was *excellent*.
John Harrison inspected this watch;
yes, he agreed, it was a fine copy.

John Harrison knew he could not begin a new watch
at this point in his life.
It was then, in 1772,
that he made a bold move.
He wrote a letter to King George III,
a man with a great interest in science.

William met with the king at Windsor Castle
and told him the bitter details
of his father's long struggle.
Later he said
that King George remarked,
"These people have been cruelly wronged. . . ."
The king also told William,
"By God, Harrison,
I will see you righted!"

The king had his own observatory in Richmond.
For several months,
King George, his assistant, and William
wound up H-5 and tested it every day at noon.
John Harrison's beautiful watch performed with little error.
But the Board of Longitude would only accept a trial at sea.
So the king took Harrison's case to Parliament.
It was there, on June 21, 1773,
that John Harrison was *finally* awarded
the remaining sum of money
for solving the longitude problem.

What a long story this has been
to tell the years of an amazing life!
John Harrison *was* a mechanical genius.
And he was a genius at a time
when bold ideas were badly needed.
From his early clocks in the village of Barrow
and from his workshop on Red Lion Square
had come the new ideas
that would create a wonderful watch—H-4—
a watch that would change the world.

Down the years,
other marine timekeepers were made
and carried aboard the many ships that sailed the oceans.
These would be called *chronometers*.
They helped tell ship captains
their exact location at sea
by giving them the correct home port time.
Now those seamen could know their longitude
as well as their latitude.

The Royal Observatory at Greenwich,
where astronomers had pinned their hopes on the stars,
became the location of the prime meridian,
zero degrees longitude.
The entire world later set its clocks
according to Greenwich mean time (GMT)
and created the time zones we use today.
And it was a *clock* that, in the end,
had given a mechanical answer
to the big problem.

John Harrison lived for three more years
after he finally won public fame.
He suffered from gout,
and his eyesight kept on failing.
Even then,
he spent time in his workshop,
tinkering,
and pondering.

Eight months before he died
at the house on Red Lion Square,
news came to London
of Captain James Cook's famous second voyage
in his ship, the *Resolution*.
During the arduous trip of three years,
from the hot tropics to the frozen Antarctic,
Larcum Kendall's watch,
the copy of Harrison's prizewinning H-4,
was used as an aid to navigation.
In the *Resolution*'s ship log,
written in his own hand,
Captain Cook called this timekeeper
"our trusty friend the Watch"
and "our never failing guide."
These words brought John Harrison much joy . . .
a joy to match his lifelong faith in his clocks.
His design of a sea watch
had changed the world in a wonderful way.

AUTHOR'S NOTE

John Harrison died on March 24, 1776. He is buried in the parish churchyard of St. John at Hampstead, not far from London. His wife, Elizabeth, died a year later, in 1777. Their cottage on the Barton Road in Barrow was lived in by Harrisons for many years. Unfortunately, it was torn down in 1968.

After John Harrison's death, his son William turned his energies toward other work. William, too, lived a long life. Upon his death in 1815, he was buried in the same tomb as his father.

H-5

Elizabeth, John Harrison's only daughter, married John Barton of London, who was also a watchmaker. Among the watches he made was an enamel portrait watch of John Harrison.

And what happened to John Harrison's wonderful sea clocks? Over the years they were stored away in odd places at Greenwich, neglected and forgotten. Then, in the 1920s, a man with the same great heart as the clockmaker from Barrow devoted most of his life to restoring the Harrison clocks to perfect working order. His name was Rupert Gould.

Today H-1, H-2, H-3, and H-4 are all on display in tall glass cases at the Royal Observatory in Greenwich, in the same building where Nevil Maskelyne worked as the Astronomer Royal and made it so difficult for a country clockmaker to win the great longitude prize. H-5 can be found on its original red satin pillow, safe in its original wood case at The Worshipful Company of Clockmakers' museum at Guildhall in London.

"It is well known to be much harder to beat out a new road,
than it is to follow that road, when made."

—William Harrison, in a letter to the Board of Longitude,

February 1764

SOME INTERESTING FACTS OF JOHN HARRISON'S LIFE STORY

✳ A LONG-CASE CLOCK can also be called a grandfather clock.

✳ THE STABLE CLOCK AT BROCKLESBY PARK is still running, keeping perfect time, almost three hundred years after John Harrison built it. It is wound every Thursday by the estate carpenter.

✳ THE ROYAL SOCIETY is a group of learned scientists in England.

✳ BENJAMIN FRANKLIN was later a recipient of the Copley Gold Medal, as was Albert Einstein.

✳ THE POCKET WATCH MADE BY JOHN JEFFERYS still exists. It was passed down to William, at Harrison's death, then to a grandson and great-grandson. Later it was sold to a jeweler in Hull who locked it in the shop's safe. This shop was destroyed in a bombing raid during World War II, and the safe was baked by fire for several days. But amazingly the watch was not lost, only damaged. It is now on display at Guildhall in London, in the Worshipful Company of Clockmakers' Museum.

✳ THE LOCATION OF THE PRIME MERIDIAN at Greenwich, England, was made official by a vote of an international conference in 1884.